THE ZEN OF WINE

David Paul Boaz

Waterfront Digital Press

ISBN:1943625107
ISBN-13:9781943625109

For Michael J. Cotter

"Such things as we have dreamed in wine, can never be told to the sober."

-    *Li Po*

O taste and see all that lives to the imagination's tongue.

- Denise Levertov

We live in two dimensions at once. The first is subjective—immediate and non-conceptual— and from this essential ground arises our objective world. Thus, in tasting, we begin with a concentrated focus of subjective sensory awareness on the palate—the nose, tongue and mouth—while intentionally bracketing, or placing in abeyance the objective or conceptual response. Following this, the conceptual or intellectual response cognizes a description of the pure sensory experience and communicates it through the gloss of wine evaluation. These

1

two apparently separate dimensions of reality, and of the organoleptic evaluation process are, at the deepest or subtlest experiential level enfolded in a prior unity. Hence, the two occur spontaneously and simultaneously at the instant of an initial sensory impression. Then, there is an apparent unfolding of this sensory process in real time as the objective world of evaluation arises from the purity of its primordial perfectly subjective ground.

Experience is evolutionary. Change is constant. Our experiences have a beginning, middle and end. In tasting, "attack" is the initial sensory impression upon the mouth and ortho nasal passage. "Evolution," or middle palate, is the sensory response to mouth aromas in the retronasal passage and to touch, the wine's tactile, taste and olfactory components. These include fruit, tannins, acidity, alcohol, extract, sweetness, glycerol, and complexity of flavors as they fan out and develop in the mouth and nose.

"Finish" is the aftertaste of these components as they linger for seconds or even minutes in the mouth and retronasal passage. Then analysis, the mental and emotional interpretation of the experience unpacks it, and gives it personal meaning which may or may not be communicated verbally.

Responding

The palate, our physical organoleptic apparatus, is a function of three sensory responses—taste, smell and touch—as well as an interpretive synthesis, the Synthetic Response. There are just four basic tastes— sweet, sour, bitter and salt. (Prove this to yourself by tasting anything at all while holding your nose.) Sweetness is detected toward the front of the tongue, sourness on the sides of the tongue, and bitterness at the rear of the tongue. All of the other nuances of taste are accomplished by the olfactory sense and the tactile/texture sense, our sense of touch. So taste, our sensory response = taste + smell + touch. Taste/flavor is reducible to smell/aroma plus texture/mouthfeel.

Thus the sensory complex that is the taste of a wine involves these Three Sensory Responses:

Olfactory: response to aromatics (the volatile esters and aldehydes);

The Four Basic Tastes: sweet, sour, bitter, salt;

Tactile: the texture, or mouth-feel of astringency, alcohol, heat, velvety smoothness, the prick of sulfur.

Then there is the fourth response, the Synthetic Response that is the cognitive/emotive synthesis of the previous three facilitating conceptual analysis and qualitative evaluation.

So the process of taste is multi-factorial involving our complex sensory response to a wine's aromatics, structure (the architecture of fruit, tannin, alcohol, extract, acidity and sweetness) and texture—the touch/mouth-feel of these structural components. Ideal response occurs at a wine temperature of 60° / 65° F.

We have seen that the purity of the tasting experience at the subjective level needs no objective analysis. It is pure, uncontrived, non-dual sensory experience given directly, as it is. This is the *satori* of the Zen of Tasting, or of any experience—pure sensory enjoyment—prior to its emergence into the world of conceptual objective description and analysis. Alas, when holistically viewed, descriptive interpretation and explanation, while separating us from the immediate beauty of the direct experience, are necessary to complete the process. As human beings we have an essential need to communicate and share our intersubjective experience. Therefore, without further lamentation, we shall continue our systematic objectification and deconstruction of an essentially subjective process.

.

Quantifying

Now that we have unabashedly objectified the purity of subjectivity that is the gift of the grape, we shall add insight to injury by quantifying its wondrous qualities.

Analysis is not tasting. The psychometric difficulties inherent in the objectification and quantification of subjective experience are legend. Yet evaluate we must. As to wine, professional or highly evolved palates (usually embodied in actual wine tasters) will agree upon a numerical value of a given wine's properties and overall quality rating at a high degree of statistical confidence. Panels of such tasters frequently differ no more than ½ point on a 20-point scale, and one point on a 100-point scale. The 20-point scales of U.C. Davis, Christies, IANO, AWS and the 100-point scales of Robert Parker and of the Wine Spectator will rate a given wine as shown in the Evaluation Form, below.

Seeing

We've seen that sensory evaluation of wine is the process of objectifying what a wine gives to the sense organs, but also to the heart. We have considered the senses of smell, taste and touch. But what of sight? What does the wine give to the eye? Besides beauty, much is revealed about a wine's age, alcohol, sweetness, body, concentration, region, varietal type and filtering by its visual appearance. There are four visual components: clarity, hue (color), saturation (intensity and depth of color), and viscosity (thickness, visual weight).

- **Clarity** (limpidity) reveals quality data in that the wine maker may have chosen to lightly fine or filter, or not to fine and filter, indicating concentration and aging potential, but also the potential for malodorous microbiological odors.

- **Hue** or color reveals information on a grape variety type, region, body and concentration (extract).

- **Saturation** is seen in the glass at the meniscus, where wine meets glass, and reveals age (both red and white wines brown with age), body, concentration, variety type and even region.

- **Viscosity** reveals body as alcohol and/or sugar. When swirled in the glass, a sweet dessert wine or a dry ripe high-alcohol wine forms legs or tears as it streams down the column of the glass. This is caused by the viscosity or surface tension of the wine interacting with the interfacial tension between the wine and glass.

Now let's put it all together.

Tasting

Pour an ounce of a good wine into a wine glass. (Life is too brief to drink bad wine.) Always hold the glass by the stem. Now hold the glass at a 45° angle to a white napkin or white table cloth. View the meniscus against this white background. See what the wine gives to the eye. Amber color at the meniscus indicates degrees of age. Now swirl the wine and ob-serve its viscosity—its legs or tears. Swirl it again to liberate its volatile elements— the aroma and perhaps, with some bottle age, the bouquet. Now place your nose into the glass. Smell what the wine immediately gives to the nose. (Note that one nostril is dominant.)

Now, breathe, smell again and observe what arises. What things do you smell? Now taste the wine and roll it over your entire pal-ate. Breathe, chew a little, and taste—but do not swallow. Now "trill" the wine to aerate and vaporize it in your mouth and involve the retronasal passage. Breathe, taste, and swallow or spit. As the wine finishes, breathe and taste but don't think, speak, or write. Just relax into it all. No need to think. No need to change anything. Here, experience and enjoy the purity and openness of this timeless moment of union of our two dimensions—subjective and objective—prior to any conceptual limit.

Let the wine speak. Now, what things do you dream in wine?

Then, practice this trans-conceptual *samadhi* without the wine.

Simply be That.

Wine Organoleptic Evaluation Form
The 20-Point Scale

Wine Number: _____

Clarity / Limpidity	Cloudy 0	Dull 0	Clear 1	Unfined 1	Brilliant 2		
Hue / Color (for type)	Too light/too dark 0	Correct 1	Light	Medium	Dark		
Saturation / Intensity	Low/medium	High 1	Age	Concentration			
Viscosity (legs/tears)	Thin	Normal	Heavy	Oily			
Aroma (fruit)	Vinous 1	Varietal 2	Enhancing 3	Oak floral spice			
Bouquet (age)	Mute 0	Enhancing intensity +1 or +2	Complexity				
Off Odors	None 0	Distracting -1 or -2	Va	Oxid	SO$_2$	Veg	Brett
Sweetness (for type)	Too low/too high/cloying 0	Correct 1	Glycerine				
Sugar	None	Low	Medium	High (+10% RS)			
Acidity	Low 0	Medium 1	Medium-full/full 1	Hot 0			
Balance (acid / fruit / alcohol)	Unbalanced	Balanced	Well-balanced 1				
Body (alcohol / extract)	Thin 0	Medium 1	Medium-full/full 1	Hot 0			
Flavor / complexity	Low 0	Medium 1	High 2	Complex	Elegant		
Astringency	Abnormal 0	Balanced 1	Soft	Hard	Harsh		
Bitterness	None/slight	Moderate	High -1				
CO$_2$ (carbonic acid)	None	Slight	Moderate	High -1			
Aftertaste / finish	Short	Lingering	Long-lingering (7–8 sec) 1				
Overall quality	Substandard 0	Standard 1	Superior 2	Terroir	Complex	Elegant	Fab
Readiness	Now	2–3 yrs	4–6 yrs	7–10 yrs	11–15 yrs	15+ yrs	

Producer: **Vintage:** **Alcohol:** **TA:**

Vineyard/Cask: **Price:** **Residual Sugar/Brix**

Negociant: **Type:** **CO$_2$:** **SO$_2$**

Importer: **Tasting Date** **Filt/Fining:** **SG:** **pH:**

Importer: **Tasting** **Locale:** **Carbonic Maceration:** **MLF:** **VA:**

My Score: **My Rank:**

Group Score: **Group Rank:** **Group First Places:**

Group Second Places: **Producer's Comments:**

Scoring
19–20	Extraordinary
17–18	Superior
15–16	Good
13–14	Standard
10–12	Substandard
<10	Flawed

David Paul Boaz

The Wine Taster's Glossary

Such things as I have dreamed in wine, can
never be told to the sober.

—Li Po

Acetic Acid (acesence): Volatile acidity (VA)
which in presence of oxygen and acetobacter
transforms alcohol to vinegar. This oxidation of
ethanol first produces acetaldehyde (maderized
odor).

Acetone/Estery: Fingernail polish odor

Acidity: With fruit, tannin and sweetness, a key
element in balance and structure. Preserves the
wine, keeps it fresh, tart, lively. Consists of
tartaric, malic, lactic, citric acid. Hot, dry
growing season and/or climate lowers acidity
and elevates brix/sugars. Total acid is usually
measured as tartaric.

Aggressive: Astringent, overly tannic, or acidic (tart), assertive, forward, youthful.

Angular/Linear: Tannic, hard, acidic from under-ripe fruit; usually a young wine.

Anis/Licorice: Aroma (bouquet) sometimes found in complex mature Burgundy and Nebbiolo.

AOC (Appellation d'Origine Contrôlee): France's official category for the top 25% of its production. Controls place of origin, grape variety, minimum alcohol, yield per hectare, certain vineyard and wine making practices.

Appley: Apple aroma in fresh young Chardonnay. Caused by malic acid.

Aroma: A young wine's nose before it develops bouquet with bottle age. Light, medium or full.

Aromatic: Fragrant, perfumed aroma of Gerwertztraminer, Riesling, Muscat and Scheurebe varieties.

Aromatics: The volatile esters and aldehydes that give a wine its aroma.

Astringent: Hard, harsh (excessive hardness), tannic, stemmy, ponderous, massive, austere, angular. Textural mouth-feel on cheeks and tongue, whereas bitterness is tasted toward the back of the tongue.

Balance: The desideratum to be wished for any wine. A harmony of fruit, tannins, acidity, alcohol, and sweetness. Well structured. In a balanced wine the "soft" components (fruit, sweetness, glycerol, alcohol) must balance the "hard" components (tannins and acidity).

Barnyard: Unclean animal smells. Damp, funky, musty earth and wood is not terroir!

Berrylike: The taste of fruit, e.g., raspberry, black cherry, blueberry, strawberry, black currant.

Body: Textural weight and mouth-feel imparted by alcohol, glycerol, sugar (if any), fruit and extract.

Botrytis: *Botrytis cinerea* or "noble rot" is a fungus that is responsible for the dehydration and resulting concentration of sugars in the great sweet wines of Germany, Barsac, Sauternes and Hungary. Botrytized wines are lusciously sweet and concentrated with high balancing acidity.

Bottle Age: Development in the bottle. Most filtered commercial wines will not improve in bottle.

Bottle Sick/Bottle Shock: An off period following bottling or shipping. May last weeks or months.

Bouquet: Complexity of aromas a maturing wine gives to the nose as it ages. May be light, medium or full (See Complexity, Aroma).

Brettanomyces ("Brett"): A yeast capable of producing malodorous earthy compounds called volatile phenols that smell like horse sweat or harness leather. Mousy smell. Brett produces acetic acid in the presence of oxygen. Present in most red wines, Brett may actually add complexity at levels below 450 micrograms per liter. Brett is not terroir!

Brix: The measure of total dissolved solids as sugars is the Brix reading of the grape or must X .55. This value equals the percent alcohol if all the sugars are fermented. Thus a reading of 20° Brix in grape juiced will yield a wine, fermented to dryness, of approximately 11% alcohol by volume. So the Brix of the must is about double the alcohol in the finished wine.

Brix may be measured in the field by a pocket-sized refractometer, or in the lab by a hydrometer.

Burned Smells: Smoky, toasty, coffee, burnt rubber

Buttery (diacetyl): The lushness of smell, taste and color in Meursault or big oaky Chardonnay.

Cabernet Sauvignon: This noble, adaptable variety makes beautiful wines in a wide variety of styles in temperate and even warm climes throughout the world. Its origins are in the great vineyards of the Medoc in Bordeaux where its greatest exemplars are produced. Cabernet seems to have been destined to be married to Merlot for on both the Left Bank of the Gironde (the Medoc) and the Right Bank (Pomerol and St- Emilion) it is blended with the softer, fruitier Merlot and Cabernet Franc. On the Right Bank, which is too cool for Cabernet, the blend is about 85% Merlot to 15% Cabernet. Cabernet in the cool climate of Bordeaux is medium bodied with pronounced tannin, deep ruby purple in color and slow maturing. Warm climate Cabernets from California's Napa Valley make an entirely different wine—rich, ripe, plumy, full-bodied and tannic. Some of it is of the highest possible excellence. Comparing the two in their youth is futile. Because the richness and forward fruit of the California wine will be more attractive in the first few years, a potentially superior Bordeaux will lose every time. And by the time the Bordeaux is mature, the California wine may be over the proverbial hill. The defining aroma for Cabernet is black currents (cassis). Great Napa Valley Cabernet often has an undertone of eucalyptus or mint.

Cava: Spanish sparkling wine fermented in the original bottle. It never approaches Champagne.

Caramel Smells: Butterscotch, honey, butter, soy sauce, chocolate, molasses

Carbonic Maceration: In red wines, the pre-fermentation of whole grape clusters before crushing. This anaerobic, intracellular fermentation without yeast allows carbon dioxide to increase in the vat, concentrating color and flavors, but not tannins. Produces bright, fruity, early maturing wines with reduced malic acid, e.g., Beaujolais and some fine Pinot Noir in France, California, Oregon, and New Zealand. After 1–3 weeks the grapes are crushed, inoculated and fermented normally.

Chardonnay: This noble grape produces the greatest dry white wines in the world—the luscious wines of Burgundy's Côte de Beaune—and their more austere Northern cousins in Chablis. California's Sonoma appellation now produces Chardonnay that rivals all but the very greatest Grand Cru wines of Corton-Charlemagne, Le Montrachet and Batard Montrachet. And California Chardonnay is improving with every vintage. In Champagne it is Chardonnay—with a little help from Pinot Noir—that produces the greatest sparkling wines on earth.

Chardonnay likes chalky soil, and the best producers use both old and new French oak to maintain that perfect balance between a richness of fruit and the complexity of restrained oak flavors. Such a wine will display a palate of crisp, nutty, smoky complexity with medium full to full body and acidity. Overtones of smoke, toast, vanilla and butterscotch are imparted by new French oak and in California are often overstated. Fresh lemony or apple tones indicate very restrained oak, or no oak.

Oak aged Chardonnay can be quite long lived. Great classic white Burgundy and California Chardonnay is fermented in small fifty-gallon old and new oak barrels and is allowed to rest upon the lees to extract flavor and complexity. Here the wine will undergo a secondary fermentation, called malolactic fermentation (MLF) which changes prickly, appley malic acid to smooth buttery lactic acid. Total acidity is thereby reduced, making the wine more accessible. Such barrel-fermented Chardonnay (BFC) loses some of its color to the lees and is therefore pale to medium yellow. BFC also loses some of its harshness and astringency, yielding a softer, rounder wine. New French (Limousin) oak and American oak are often too intrusive. Thus the use of older oak or a mixture of old and new as the wine is racked between the two.

In Chablis we taste an entirely different Chardonnay. Chablis is famous for its pale, greenish yellow color, austere, steely, mineral-stoney bouquet, crisp, lean, subtle yet complex palate and long complex finish. The best Chablis is BFC, but oak is highly restrained. The Northern clime, short growing season and chalky Kimmeridgean soils produce very high acidity that in a Grand Cru Chablis translates to an extremely long-lived wine. Premiers Cru and Grand Cru Chablis are entirely different wines as to quality, richness, complexity. The bouquet and flowers that develop in a Grand Cru Les Clos, Blanchot or Valmur from a great vintage after ten years of bottle age are the very quintessence of the gift of the Chardonnay grape.

Chocolatey: Mocha, coffee aroma in some young vintage and ruby ports, Cabernet, and Merlot

Clarity: May be cloudy, dull, clear or brilliant. Bright filtered wines improve little in the bottle.

Clean: A wine with no faults. Usually a young, fresh wine.

Closed: Backward, aromas and flavors not accessible. May open up in the glass, or overnight.

Cloying: High sweetness/sugar without the acidity to balance it. Syrupy.

Color/Hue: *Reds*—purple, ruby purple, brick red, garnet or ruby red, tawny, amber. *Whites*—colorless, green tinge, pale yellow, yellow gold, gold amber (see Hue, Saturation).

Complexity: Harmony of aromas, flavors, depth, intensity, richness. Flavors of berries, herbs, spices, tobacco, pepper, cedar, mint. Intensity of flavors may be light, medium or full. Contributing variables to complexity are age, style, varietal character, balance and finish (see Balance).

Complexity in Chardonnay: Buttery, vanillin, lemony, apples, pears, toasted oak, yeast, minerals, chalky, flinty, honeysuckle, jasmine, honey. Butter, vanillin, toast, honey are due to oak aging.

Concentrated: Rich, ripe, intense, luscious fruit, plumy, fleshy, viscous; density of fruit, extract, unctuous. Fruit does not imply sweetness but may be "sweetish" from fruit and glycerol.

Corked: Musty cork smell due to a rotten cork. Caused by TCA (trichloranisole).

DOCG (Denominazione di Origine Controllata e Garantita): DOC controls about what France's AOC laws control. Above this, DOCG is granted only to 11 wines. The greatest are: Barolo, Brunello di Montalcino, Barbaresco, Vino Nobile di Montepulciano, and Chianti Classico.

Developed: Maturity stage, contrasted with underdeveloped, well developed (mature, balanced), and over-developed (falling apart). Big, full bodied, complex wines may develop in the glass or bottle overnight.

Dumb: Underdeveloped stage with the potential for development. Some may not recover.

Earthy: Complexity as truffles, mushrooms, musty, tarry, leathery, woody.

Eucalyptus: Minty bouquet in Cabernet, especially California's Napa Valley from Eucalyptus trees.

Extract: The textural component that includes a wine's dissolved solids—sugars, glycerol, tannins and pigments that contribute to body, character and complexity.

Finish (aftertaste): Length, persistence of flavor and fragrance in the nose and mouth after the wine is swallowed or spit. May be short, lingering or long lingering.

Flavor Intensity: The intensity of enhancing flavors and complexity. May be light, medium, or full.

Forward: Aromatic, open, revealing its charms. In youth, lacking depth and complexity.

Fresh: Lively, tart, good acidity, (see Clean).

Full-Bodied: Full concentration of fruit, glycerol, alcohol and extract (+ 13.5 alc), full in the mouth, with weight, backbone, power, tannic, firm, but not heavy, massive or ponderous.

Floral Smells: Violet, rose, orange blossom.

Fruity Smells: Citrus, berry, cherry, peach, apple, pineapple, melon, banana, raisin, prune, fig.

Gassy: Presence of dissolved carbon dioxide (CO_2) as carbonic acid (H_2CO_3). May be due to secondary fermentation in the bottle. May or may not dissipate as wine is swirled in the glass.

Glycerol (glycerin): A by-product of fermentation. Imparts a slightly sweet, viscous impression on the palate without the presence of sugar.

Grip: Forward, full, assertive complex of "masculine" qualities in a big red wine or Port.

Grace and Finesse: Elegance, silky, velvet, soft, round, delicate, feminine qualities. (see Breed)

Herbaceous: Basil, lavender, rosemary, fennel aromas.

Hot: Alcohol too high for wine type, style or structure. Insufficient fruit and extract to balance alcohol.

Hue/Saturation: Hue is the color, saturation is the depth, limpidity and brilliance of the color, seen at the meniscus or rim at 45° to a white background (see Color, Hue).

Hydrogen Sulfide (H_2S): Mercaptan, nitrogen reduction, rubbery, sewage/rotten egg smell.

Light-Bodied: Lighter concentration of glycerol, alcohol, extract; lean and light on the palate.

Malolactic Fermentation (MLF): This desirable secondary fermentation of red or white wine in the barrel or bottle converts the harshness of malic acid to softer, buttery lactic acid and reduces the total acidity (TA), yielding a softer, rounder, more approachable wine.

Mature: At plateau, round, complex, balanced. The end of development, but before decline.

Mercaptan: Chemical compound that produces hydrogen sulfide (H_2S) or rotten egg/sewage smell.

Merlot: This marvelous supple variety produces some of the greatest, most expensive red wines in the world, including the incomparable Chateau Pétrus of Pomerol, and Chateau Ausone in St-Emilion. Merlot wines can be wonderfully soft, rich, plumy, sweetish yet spicy with a deep color, high alcohol and extract, yet low tannin and astringency. Fine Merlot has a textural robe of velvet and a ripe but spicy, complex aroma. There are more hectares under Merlot vines in Bordeaux than any other variety, including Cabernet. California's Napa and Sonoma regions are now producing some beautiful, approachable Merlots that should improve in bottle for 8 to 10 years or more.

Méthode Tratitionelle or Méthode Champenois: Champagne or other quality sparkling wine fermented in its original bottle. Yields superior wine to the transfer or to the Charmat bulk process.

Microbiological Smells: Mousy, horsey, sweaty leather, sauerkraut. Caused by Brett, TCA, tourne.

Mineral Smell: Steely undertones of chalk, iron, metal, flint (Chablis, Riesling, Cabernet)

Mousse: The fine, creamy, mousse-like head and mouth-feel of fine Champagne.

Mouth-feel: see Texture.

Musty: Mildew, moldy. Not *terroir*!

Nebbiolo: Undistinguished elsewhere, in the terroir of Italy's Piedmont, Nebbiolo makes the fabulous wines of Barolo, Barbaresco and Gattinara. Thick skinned, deep colored, tannic and long lived, Nebbiolo is renowned for its complex aromas often described with such epithets as violets, truffles, mint, tar, anise and prunes. Bitter and unapproachable in their youth.

Nose: Aroma or bouquet. What the wine gives to the nose (see Aroma, Bouquet).

Nutty: Aroma and/or flavor of roasted nuts.

Oxidized: Stale, cooked, sherry-like smell and taste of acetaldehyde due to the oxidation of phenolics (pulp, juice) that converts ethanol to acetaldehyde. Also causes browning. Maderization.

Palate: 1. The complex of smell, taste, and touch or texture. 2. The overall taste impression of a wine, or a specific aspect on the palate, as in "a balanced palate," or "rich fruit on the palate."

Papery: Wet cardboard odor.

Peachy: Bouquet of peaches in Viognier and the ripe *Prädikat* wines of Germany's Mosel region.

Petroleum (Petrol): Aroma undertone sometimes found in *Prädikat* Rhinegau, Port, Shiraz.

Philosophical Considerations: Is the tasting process objective or subjective? Is there an objective quality standard for wine evaluation; or is it ultimately a matter of subjective preference? Clearly, the answer to both of these questions is that both objective and subjective factors are always present.
      Our sensory response to the specific chemical compounds present in a wine—sugars, acids, tannins, acetic acid—is objective. These compounds are universally perceived and objectively, chemically measured.

However, qualities requiring an evaluation of quality—balance, harmony, complexity of flavors, finesse, elegance, breed—involve subjective judgments of value. Yet with highly trained tasters, even these qualities can be objectified to a very high degree of statistical confidence. Thus tasting involves both objective sensory perception, and subjective judgments of quality, and upon reflection, these seem to occur spontaneously and simultaneously. That is, objectivity and subjectivity are here a prior unity.

Being Here. Broadly construed, the history of the Western Tradition has been an attempt to reduce subjective experience—feeling, emotion, spirit—to objective, external material substance (reductionism, scientific materialism).

The history of the Eastern Tradition has been an attempt to reduce objective experience—what appears empirically to the senses—to subjective, inner contemplative and religious experience. The truth of the matter, and the truth of the feeling is that we live in these two worlds at once! Objective and subjective are always, already a prior unity. These are the two cognitive dimensions that we are. All experience arises through, and is relative (related) to that unity.

In the 21st Century, East meets West, and the two are ultimately realized to coexist in a vast interdependent matrix wherein the knowing, tasting subject and our perceived vinous object can no longer be epistemologically or ontologically separated.

Therefore, let us surrender our dualistic bias and argument in favor of one or the other of these polarities, and embrace the prior unbounded whole, all the while objectively analyzing and evaluating, trans-concepually, subjectively surrendering—and most of all enjoying—the sublime gift that a conscious life with a bit of wine can be.

Phylloxera: A root louse that nearly annihilated Vinifera in Europe. Vineyards were saved by grafting European Vinifera scions to phylloxera-resistant American rootstock. Phylloxera is now a problem in the U.S.

Pinot Noir: Thin-skinned, capricious, early ripening, always challenging, Pinot Noir produces the majestic red wines of Burgundy's Côte d'Or. At their best, these wines are, arguably, the greatest dry red wines in the world. California's foggy coastal appellations (Sonoma's Russian River Valley, Santa

Barbara's Santa Rita Hills, Monterey's Santa Lucia Highlands) and Oregon's Willamette Valley now rival all but the greatest wines of Burgundy's Côte de Nuits. The palate of great Pinot Noir is of rich, ripe, berry-like fruit, sweetish, soft, silky, velvety and elegant. Pinot Noir is approachable earlier than the bigger reds of Bordeaux (Cabernet), the full-bodied wines of the Rhone (Syrah), Italy's Piedmont (Nebbiolo) and Tuscany (Sangiovese). Most Pinot Noir should be consumed within 4 to 8 years. A great Côte de Nuits will last 18–20 years or longer. Often light in color, Pinot Noir's delicate scent is berry-like with overtones of black cherries, raspberries, strawberries, and in its youth, violets, with earthy musky, spicy, complexity at maturity. Quality Pinot Noir will see 1-2 years in older French Limousin or Troncais oak. Oak flavors are restrained. Malolactic fermentation is encouraged.

Piquant: Fresh, tartness and acidity in, for example, the Mosel wines of Germany.

Ponderous: Heavy-bodied, alcohol out of balance with acidity and fruit, probably to the very end.

Port: This is the great sweet dessert wine grown and made in the Douro Valley in northern Portugal. It is made from the Touriga Nacional or the Tinta Cão grape varieties. *Caveat*: If it's not from Portugal, it's not Port. Non-Portugal "ports" can be decent dessert wines, but cannot compare to older Tawnies or LBV, let alone vintage port.

Ruby Port: young cask-aged (not bottle aged) for two or three years. Simple filtered blends. Non-complex, berry-like aroma and flavors offer a charming, inexpensive dessert wine. Cutting calories? Try one once of Ruby Port, or better yet a ten year old Tawny, and forget the dessert.

Tawny Port: cask-aged for 10, 20 or 30 years. Tawny *Reserva* spends seven years or more in wood. Red amber in color. Twenty or thirty year old Tawny resembles a mature vintage port, and is nearly as expensive. Ten year old Tawny Port can represent excellent price/value. Inexpensive Tawny is two or three years old, usually has seen no wood, is made from lighter grapes that do not achieve the ripeness of Ruby Ports, and are often blended with pedestrian white port. Still, a nice aperitif when chilled, or on the rocks. Ruby and Tawny

Port is consumed in the Douro Valley over ice. It makes a delightful summer cooler!

Late Bottled Vintage (LBV): cask-aged wood port, blended and bottled at 4 to 6 years after its vintage. Will not improve much in bottle, and may throw a little sediment. It can be very good, but it's not Vintage Port.

Vintage Port: bottle-aged port. Only the finest vintages are declared by the producers. Vintages are declared on average thrice a decade. Blended and bottled 2–3 years after its vintage. This deep purple nectar requires 25 to 30 years in bottle, in your cellar, to mature. It will continue to improve for another 25 to 30 years, or more. Can't wait? Drink it in ten years!

Major Port shippers are Fonseca, Dow, Taylor Fladgate, Sandeman, Graham, Cockburn, Croft, and Warre. Will throw much sediment at maturity, so it must be carefully decanted using cheese cloth or fine mesh, and a backlight. Drink at 65°f, alone, or with good pastry, creme brulee, berries and cream, or chocolate. Unquestionably the greatest red dessert wine in the galaxy! Fabulous!

Pricked: Acetic acid or volatile acidity odor that first marks a wine's descent into vinegar.

Pungent: Assertive spice and complexity as volatile acidity in old sherry, Tawny Port, Madeira, Shiraz. If VA becomes too high (acetic acid/vinegar) the wine is spoiled.

Purity: The very best varietal character or other defining characteristic.

Qualitätswein mit Prädikat **(QmP):** "Quality wine with special designations," Germany's quality Riesling wine hierarchy. Quality is based upon ripeness and ranges from simple *Qualitätswein (QbA)* to the *prädikat* wines, namely, *Kabinett, Spätlese, Auslese, Beerenauslese (BA), Trockenbeerenauslese (TBA)* and *Eiswein*. The last three are the great sweet botrytized wines infected with the "noble rot" botrytis cinerea. *Eiswein*, picked and crushed frozen, concentrates sugar, acid and extract. Rare and wonderful.

Raisiny: Smell of dried or overripe grapes in some late harvest and hot climate wines, and inexpensive Ruby and Tawny Ports.

Riesling: At the pinnacle of noble Vinifera varieties, Riesling is the most versatile. Grown successfully in every wine producing region of the world, it produces superb wines across the spectrum of dry to sweet to very sweet dessert wines. Riesling shines in Alsace as dry wine under the guidance of the great producers Trimbach and Hugel. In the Reingau and Mosel regions of Germany it produces not only fine dry (trocken) wines, but the charming *Spätlese* and the luscious *Auslese,* and the fabulous nectar of the sweet late harvest botrytis wines known as *Beerenauslese* (BA) and *Trokenbeerenauslese* (TBA) that improve in bottle almost forever. Riesling is quite sensitive to its *terroir* and expresses it very specifically throughout its global reach. Its color ranges from pale greenish straw to deep gold at maturity. Its aroma is delicate, perfumed, fresh, clean, floral, and in the late harvest wines, honeyed and muscat-scented. Riesling in Germany is a cold climate wine that struggles with the elements to ripen. It is therefore low in alcohol (7–9%) and high in refreshing acidity. The slightly sweet *Kabinett* and *Spätlese* make the perfect aperitif, or a summertime picnic wine. The palate of a well-made Mosel is steely with light body, fresh, crisp, fruity acidity that perfectly balances the sweetness, and a clean, refreshing and lingering finish. Rheingau has slightly more body. *Auslese* is sweeter than *Spätlese*. BA and TBA are rich, unctuous, sweet without being cloying, and complex with a high balancing acidity that leaves a clean long finish. Enjoy at 45 to 55°f, alone or with dessert. These wines, with the great wines of Sauternes and Barsac, are indisputably the greatest sweet white wines in the cosmos!

Resinous: Scents of oak, cedar, pine, eucalyptus. In Greek Retsina it's actually resin.

Residual Sugar: Percent sugar remaining in finished wine upon the termination of fermentation.

Sangiovese: Only in the great wines of Tuscany does this noble variety shine. In Brunello di Montalcino, Vino Nobile de Montepulciano and Chianti Classico, Sangiovese produces classic, full-bodied wines of high acidity and medium to deep ruby color. These wines are quite astringent in their youth, often with some bitterness. They age well and are long lived. Often not approachable in their youth.

Sekt: German sparkling wine. With the exception of some *Deutscher Sekt* bA, quite common.

Sèmillon: This is the noble variety that produces the marvelous (and expensive) dessert wines of Bordeaux' Sauternes and Barsac in the Graves region. As with the late harvest Rieslings, it is Botrytis cinerea ("noble rot") that dehydrates and concentrates the sugar in the grapes and imparts the ripe, honeyed scent and the capacity to improve in the bottle for decades. In Sauternes and Barsac, Sèmillon is blended with 15 to 20% Sauvignon Blanc. The supreme exemplars of the Sèmillon grape are the Grand Cru and the Premiers Cru wines. These luscious sweet wines are full-bodied and balanced by very high acidity. The palate is creamy and nutty, of apricot and honey. The lone Grand Cru, the incomparable Chateau d'Yquem (Sauternes) is indisputably the most famous white dessert wine in the world, and the greatest French sweet wine. The great Premiers Cru of the region are Climens (Barsac) and Coutet (Barsac), Rieussec (Sauternes) and Suduiraut (Sauternes). The latter two often represent excellent price/value.

Soft: Round, drinkable, quaffable, supple, silky. Alcohol/extract/sugar (softness) must balance acidity/astringency (hardness).

Spicy: Scents of black pepper, anise, cedar, pine, mint, eucalyptus, tobacco, cinnamon, smoke.

Spritz: Carbonic acid (dissolved CO_2) and/or tartaric acid in a fresh young wine. *Spritzig* in Germany.

Steely: White wine with high acidity and mineral overtones, e.g., firm, lean, stony Chablis.

Stemmy: Bitterness imparted to a wine macerated on the stems.

Structure: The architecture of fruit, tannins, alcohol, extract, acidity and sweetness. A harmonious structure is the balance of these components wherein "hard" elements (tannins and acid) do not overwhelm "soft" elements (alcohol, sweetness, fruit). (See Balance, Complexity).

Subtle: Cloaked, nuanced, restrained complexity.

Sugared: Sweetish smell/taste of a *chaptalized* wine (sugar added to juice or must).

Sulfur: Sulfur dioxide (SO_2, burnt match) is the prickly feel in nose and throat. Usually swirls off in the glass. Sulfur dioxide is almost universally used in wine making as a preservative and disinfectant. Hydrogen sulfide

(H_2S) is the rotten egg/sewage odor of a ruined wine. Low levels may swirl off.

Syrah: In the terroir of Northern Rhone, in the fabulous wines of Côte Rôtie, Hermitage, Crozes Hermitage, St. Joseph and Cornas, Syrah is inky dark purple, tannic and astringent. Full-bodied with its characteristic black pepper, smoky aromas and extremely dry finish, these wines need 5 to 8 years of bottle age, and will improve much longer. In Australia Syrah is known as Shiraz and whether in the cool *terroir* of Coonawarra or in the heat of the Barossa Valley it makes excellent wines of quite different characters than those of the Rhone. Shiraz/Syrah is cultivated successfully in California, Washington State, Spain, and South Africa. In the Southern Rhone it is blended with Grenache to add spiciness, texture and color to the great wines of Châteauneuf-du-Pape.

Tartrate Crystals (*Weinstein*): Harmless crystals of tartaric acid precipitate. Cold stabilization is widely used—for marketing reasons—to prevent them.

Tart: Acidic, lean, green, unripe. Not necessarily a flaw.

Taste: Taste involves our sensory response to a wine's Aromatics (volatile esters and aldehydes), Structure (the architecture of fruit, tannins, alcohol, extract, acidity, sweetness, and Texture or Mouth-feel (astringency, heat, velvet). Thus there are three basic sensory responses:

1. *Olfactory*
2. *The Four Basic Tastes (sweet, sour, bitter, salt) and recently, umami*
3. *Tactile, or touch*
4. *A fourth response, the Synthetic Response, is a cognitive / emotive synthesis of these three that facilitates evaluation.*

Taste Memory: The ability to remember and describe specific characteristics of a wine when reading notes, recalling it or re-tasting it. "Trigger words" help (e.g. black currants for Cabernet).

Tears (legs): A high viscosity (high alcohol, high sugar, or both) wine forms tears or legs as it streams down the column of a glass. It is caused by surface tension of the wine and interfacial tension between the wine and the glass as alcohol evaporates.

Tempranillo: Spain's noble red variety ripens early and produces firm, deeply colored, low acidity, and light to medium bodied wines that when aged in American oak make charming, soft, complex, early drinking wines that age well. In the Ribera del Duero, Rioja, Navarra and Penedes viticultural areas Tempranillo is known as Tinta Fino or Ull de Llebre. In Portugal it is Tinta Roriz.

Terroir: Multi-factorial term representing the variables governing the natural environment of a viticultural site as they affect wine: climate, microclimate, weather, sunlight, soil composition, slope/drainage/topography and altitude. Overrated in determining final character wherein the producer is primary, followed by vintage, appellation and then *terroir*. Vinifera varieties transmit *terroir* to varying degrees. For example, Riesling, Nebbiolo and Pinot Noir reflect their *terroir* to a high degree, e.g., Reisling in the Mosel and Resiling in California are entirely different wines. At the subtlest level *terroir* is the history and culture of a people and their cuisine. In sociocultural spacetime, wine follows cuisine.

Texture: Mouth-feel or tactile response to a wine's structural components, i.e., astringency, extract, viscosity, temperature, heat (alcohol), fizziness. Great wines have an ineffable textural robe.

Thin: Lean, hollow, shallow, dilute, over-cropped, under-ripe, lack of fruit and flavor.

Tired: Past plateau, oxidized, vapid, falling apart, over the proverbial hill.

Touriga Nacional: This varietal of the great sweet wines of Portugal (Port) also produces long lived, still, dry wines of excellent character, complexity, depth of flavor and color.

Ullage: Dead air space in bottle or cask that may cause oxidation if not topped up or re-corked.

Unfined/Unfiltered: Enhances a wine's capacity to improve after bottling. Most, but not all, commercial wines are overly fined, filtered and sulfured and will improve little in the bottle.

Umami: Recently discovered fifth taste (after sweet, sour, bitter, and salt). Reminiscent of MSG.

Vanilla: Desirable smell derived from aging in oak casks or barrels.

THE ZEN OF WINE

Varietal Aroma: The characteristic aroma of the grape variety used to make the wine.

Vegetal: Unpleasant herbaceousness, leafy, grassy, unripe, green. May add complexity in some mature wines (e.g. Pinot Noir and Livermore Valley [California] Cabernet).

Vegetal Smells: Grassy, bell pepper, eucalyptus, mint, asparagus, olive, artichoke, hay, tea, tobacco.

Vinuous: A blended wine not expressing specific varietal character. May be simple or exceptional.

Vitis Vinifera: Genus and species from which the noble wine grape varieties descend. Does not include the indigenous American species *Vitus Labrusca* (Concord grapes).

Volatile Acidity (VA): Acetic acid. Odor of ethyl acetate. In air the bacterium acetobacter turns alcohol (ethanol) to vinegar. Undetectable at low levels, it is present in all wines (see Ascetic Acid).

Woody/Oaky Toasty: Aroma or bouquet secondary to aging in charred or new oak barrels

Yeasty: Desirable characteristic of Champagne, bottle-fermented sparkling wines and some German wines. A flaw in most still wine caused by secondary fermentation in bottle.

Notes

* 9 7 8 1 9 4 3 6 2 5 1 0 9 *